APPLE
INTELLIGENCE
TECH REVIEW

A Comprehensive Guide for
Embracing Cutting-Edge AI
Capabilities and Revolutionizing
Your Digital Experience

Geoffrey Derby

COPYRIGHT

CONTENT

3

INTRODUCTION

Apple Intelligence represents a groundbreaking leap in the realm of artificial intelligence, seamlessly integrating advanced AI capabilities into the Apple ecosystem. Officially unveiled on June 10, 2024, at WWDC 2024, this innovative platform is set to revolutionize the user experience across iOS 18, iPadOS 18, and macOS Sequoia, which were announced concurrently.

This transformative platform harnesses the power of both on-device and server processing, ensuring efficient and robust performance. A significant highlight of Apple Intelligence is its integration with

OpenAI's ChatGPT, enhancing Siri's capabilities by allowing it to delegate complex user queries to ChatGPT when necessary. This synergy between Apple's intuitive design and OpenAI's conversational expertise marks a pivotal moment in AI evolution.

The journey to Apple Intelligence began with Apple's strategic acquisition of Perceptio in October 2015, a company known for its proficiency in on-device AI modeling. This acquisition was a critical step in Apple's mission to develop cutting-edge AI technology while maintaining the highest standards of privacy and security. Despite the initial secrecy surrounding Apple's AI endeavors, which even dissuaded some academic collaborations, the company's dedication to innovation has culminated in the sophisticated AI platform we see today.

Apple Intelligence is compatible with a range of devices equipped with Apple's M-series silicon processors. This includes Macs such as the MacBook Air (M1, 2020) and later, MacBook Pro (M1, 2020) and later, Mac mini (M1, 2020) and later, Mac Pro (M2 Ultra, 2023), Mac Studio (M1 Pro, 2022) and later, and iMac (M1, 2021) and later. iPads like the iPad Air (M1, 5th generation) and later and iPad Pro (M1, 5th generation) and later are also supported. Additionally, all iPhones with the A17 Pro or later, starting with the iPhone 15 Pro and iPhone 15 Pro Max, are capable of utilizing Apple Intelligence.

This book aims to explore the myriad facets of Apple Intelligence, from its development and integration to its practical applications and future potential. Join us as we delve into the intricacies of this cutting-edge technology and uncover how Apple Intelligence is poised to redefine our interaction with devices in an increasingly intelligent world.

Part I

Apple Sets a New Benchmark for AI Privacy with Apple Intelligence

Apple has unveiled a revolutionary step forward in the realm of personal technology with the introduction of Apple Intelligence. This state-of-the-art personal intelligence system, designed specifically for iPhone, iPad, and Mac, combines the formidable capabilities of generative models with the nuanced understanding of personal context.

This synergy results in intelligence that is not only highly useful but also extraordinarily relevant to each individual user.

Apple Intelligence is meticulously integrated into the latest operating systems—iOS 18, iPadOS 18, and macOS Sequoia. By leveraging the immense processing power of Apple silicon, this system excels at comprehending and generating both language and images, seamlessly executing a multitude of actions across various applications. Moreover, it draws upon personal context to simplify and accelerate a wide array of everyday tasks, enhancing the user experience in unprecedented ways.

A standout feature of Apple Intelligence is its commitment to privacy, embodied in the innovative Private Cloud Compute. This feature represents a significant advancement in AI technology, setting a new standard for privacy. It enables a dynamic and flexible scaling of computational capacity, balancing the workload between on-device processing and larger, server-based models. These models run on dedicated Apple silicon servers, ensuring that the computational demands are met efficiently without compromising user privacy.

Through this sophisticated balance, Apple Intelligence not only provides powerful and relevant insights but also ensures that users' data remains secure. The system's ability to flexibly shift computational tasks between local and server-based resources means that users can enjoy the benefits of advanced AI without sacrificing their privacy. Apple's dedication to privacy and user-centric design shines through in this latest innovation, setting a new benchmark in the industry and paving the way for future advancements in personal intelligence systems.

With Apple Intelligence, the company continues to push the boundaries of what personal technology can achieve, offering tools that are deeply integrated into users' daily lives and workflows. This system not only understands and responds to individual needs but also anticipates them, providing a seamless, intuitive, and highly personalized experience. As Apple sets a new standard for privacy in AI, it reaffirms its commitment to creating technology that is both powerful and respectful of users' personal data.

"We're excited to unveil a groundbreaking chapter in Apple's legacy of innovation. Apple Intelligence is set to revolutionize the capabilities of our products and enhance the experiences they provide to our users," said Tim Cook, Apple's CEO.

"Our distinctive approach merges the power of generative AI with the unique personal context of each user, delivering intelligence that is genuinely helpful and relevant. This system accesses and processes information in a way that is completely private and secure, empowering users to focus on what matters most to them. This is AI designed and executed as only Apple can, and we eagerly anticipate users discovering the incredible possibilities it unlocks."

Part II

New Capabilities for Lingual Understanding and Creation

Apple Intelligence introduces groundbreaking ways for users to enhance their writing skills and communicate more effectively. This innovation comes with new systemwide Writing Tools integrated into iOS 18, iPadOS 18, and macOS Sequoia, allowing users to rewrite, proofread, and summarize text across various applications, including Mail, Notes, Pages, and even third-party apps.

These Writing Tools are designed to assist users in a multitude of writing scenarios.

Whether it's tidying up class notes, ensuring a blog post reads perfectly, or crafting a meticulously worded email, Apple Intelligence helps users feel more confident in their writing. The Rewrite feature empowers users to choose from different versions of their text, adjusting the tone and style to suit the specific audience and purpose. This could range from refining a cover letter for a job application to infusing humor and creativity into a party invitation. With Rewrite, users can always find the right words for any occasion.

Proofread is another powerful tool within Apple Intelligence, designed to check grammar, word choice, and sentence structure. It suggests edits along with detailed explanations, enabling users to review and understand the changes before accepting them. This feature ensures that every piece of writing is polished and professional, enhancing clarity and precision.

Additionally, the Summarize feature provides a quick and efficient way to condense lengthy texts. Users can select any text and have it summarized into a digestible paragraph, bulleted key points, a table, or a list. This functionality is incredibly useful for creating concise overviews, extracting key information, or generating summaries for quick reference.

Overall, Apple Intelligence's Writing Tools are crafted to support and enhance users' writing experiences across a variety of contexts and applications. With these tools, Apple continues to push the boundaries of personal technology, providing users with intelligent solutions that simplify and improve their daily tasks.

Mail Made Effortless: Stay on Top of Emails with Priority Messages and Smart Features

In Mail, managing emails has become remarkably straightforward. The new Priority Messages section at the top of the inbox highlights the most urgent emails, such as same-day dinner invitations or boarding passes, ensuring that users never miss critical information. Instead of merely previewing the first few lines of each email, users can now see concise summaries without needing to open each message. For lengthy email threads, a single tap reveals the most pertinent details, making it easier to keep track of conversations. Additionally, Smart Reply offers quick response suggestions and identifies questions within an email to ensure comprehensive replies.

Enhanced Notifications: Prioritizing What Matters Most

Apple Intelligence extends its deep understanding of language to Notifications as well. Priority Notifications appear at the top of the stack, bringing the most important alerts to immediate attention. Summaries of notifications help users quickly scan through long or grouped notifications, displaying key details directly on the Lock Screen, such as updates from an active group chat. The new Reduce Interruptions feature, part of the Focus settings, ensures that users stay present in their activities by surfacing only the notifications that might need immediate attention, like a text message about an early pickup from daycare.

Notes and Phone Apps: Advanced Audio Features

The Notes and Phone apps now include powerful audio capabilities. Users can record, transcribe, and summarize audio with ease. When a recording is initiated during a phone call, all participants are automatically notified. Once the call concludes, Apple Intelligence generates a summary, capturing the key points discussed. This feature is particularly useful for recalling important details from meetings, interviews, or any significant conversation.

These enhancements across Mail, Notifications, Notes, and Phone apps illustrate Apple's commitment to improving user experience through intelligent and intuitive design. With Apple Intelligence, users can stay organized, respond efficiently, and focus on what truly matters in their daily lives.

Part III

New Image Creation Capabilities for Enhanced Communication and Self-Expression

Apple Intelligence introduces thrilling new image creation features designed to empower users in communicating and expressing themselves more creatively. With the innovative Image Playground, users can generate captivating images in seconds, selecting from three distinct styles: Animation, Illustration, or Sketch. This user-friendly tool is seamlessly integrated into various apps, including Messages, and is also available as a standalone app, perfect for exploring and experimenting with diverse concepts and styles. Importantly, all images are created directly on the device, providing users with the freedom to experiment and create as many images as they desire without concerns about privacy or data security.

Image Playground: A Canvas for Creativity

Image Playground offers a wide array of creative possibilities. Users can choose from an extensive range of concepts categorized into themes, costumes, accessories, and places. By typing a description, they can define the image they envision, and even include someone from their personal photo library to personalize their creation further. Once the elements are chosen, users can pick their preferred style—whether it's the dynamic flair of Animation, the detailed artistry of Illustration, or the simple elegance of Sketch.

This feature is designed to be accessible and fun, encouraging users to explore their creativity and share their unique visual stories with friends and family. Whether it's crafting a whimsical scene for a birthday message, designing a custom illustration for a blog post, or creating a playful sketch for social media, Image Playground makes the process enjoyable and straightforward.

Empowering Users with On-Device Creation

All image creation processes happen on the device itself, ensuring that users' privacy is maintained and their data remains secure. This on-device capability allows users to freely experiment with different ideas and styles without any limitations, fostering an environment where creativity can flourish without compromise.

Revolutionizing Communication and Self-Expression

Apple Intelligence's image creation capabilities revolutionize the way users communicate and express themselves. By integrating advanced tools like Image

Playground into everyday apps and offering a dedicated platform for more extensive experimentation, Apple empowers users to convey their messages and emotions visually, in ways that are engaging, personalized, and fun. This commitment to enhancing user experience through innovative technology underscores Apple's dedication to pushing the boundaries of what personal devices can achieve, making creativity more accessible and enjoyable for everyone.

Enhancing Visual Communication Across Apple Apps

With the Image Playground feature in Messages, users can effortlessly create fun images for their friends, making conversations more engaging and visually appealing. This experience is further enhanced by personalized suggested concepts tailored to the conversation. For instance, if a user is chatting with a group about an upcoming hiking trip, they will see suggestions related to their friends, the destination, and the activity. This makes the image creation process not only quicker but also more relevant and connected to the ongoing discussion.

Elevate Your Notes with Image Playground

In the Notes app, Image Playground can be accessed via the new Image Wand in the Apple Pencil tool palette. This feature transforms notes into more visually engaging documents. Users can convert rough sketches into delightful, polished images or create new images by selecting empty spaces, utilizing context from the surrounding text. This makes notes more dynamic and visually appealing, adding a creative touch to everyday tasks.

Integration Across Apple's Ecosystem

Image Playground's capabilities extend beyond Messages and Notes. It is integrated into apps like Keynote, Freeform, and Pages, where users can enhance their presentations, brainstorming sessions, and documents with creative visuals. Third-party apps can also adopt the new Image Playground API, bringing these powerful image creation tools to an even broader range of applications.

Personalized and Contextual Image Suggestions

By integrating Image Playground across various apps, Apple ensures that users have consistent access to creative tools that are both powerful and intuitive. Personalized suggestions based on conversation context in Messages streamline the process of creating relevant images. This feature leverages the power of Apple Intelligence to understand and anticipate users' needs, making the creative process more efficient and enjoyable.

Creative Freedom with On-Device Processing

All image creation is handled on-device, ensuring privacy and security while allowing unlimited experimentation. Users can explore different concepts, styles, and ideas without any constraints, fostering an environment where creativity can thrive.

A New Standard in Visual Communication

Apple's integration of Image Playground into its suite of applications underscores its commitment to enhancing user experiences through innovative technology. By making image creation tools accessible and intuitive, Apple enables users to communicate and express themselves more vividly and creatively. This comprehensive approach to visual communication ensures that users can easily incorporate fun, personalized images into their daily interactions and tasks, setting a new standard for creativity and engagement across digital platforms.

Genmoji Creation to Fit Any Situation

Taking emoji to an entirely new level, users can create an original Genmoji to express themselves. By simply typing a description, their Genmoji appears, along with additional options. Users can even create Genmoji of friends and family based on their photos. Just like emoji, Genmoji can be added inline to messages, or shared as a sticker or reaction in a Tapback.

New Features in Photos Give Users More Control

Enhanced Photo and Video Search with Apple Intelligence

Apple Intelligence revolutionizes the way users search for photos and videos, making it more convenient and intuitive. With natural language processing, users can find specific photos by simply describing them. For instance, typing "Maya skateboarding in a tie-dye shirt" or "Katie with stickers on her face" will quickly locate those exact images. Video search becomes equally powerful, allowing users to pinpoint specific moments within clips, enabling them to jump directly to the relevant segment without manually scrubbing through the footage.

Clean Up Tool for Perfect Photos

The new Clean Up tool is another standout feature of Apple Intelligence. This tool can identify and remove distracting objects in the background of a photo without unintentionally altering the main subject. This ensures that users can perfect their images, maintaining focus on the primary subject while eliminating any unwanted elements seamlessly.

Crafting Personalized Memories with Apple Intelligence

With the Memories feature, users can easily create personalized stories from their photos and videos. By simply typing a description of the desired memory, Apple Intelligence uses its advanced language and image understanding capabilities to select the best photos and videos that match the description.

It then crafts a storyline with chapters based on themes identified from the photos, arranging them into a cohesive movie with a clear narrative arc. To enhance the experience, users receive song suggestions from Apple Music that perfectly complement the memory.

Privacy at the Forefront

As with all Apple Intelligence features, privacy is a top priority. Users' photos and videos are kept private on their devices and are not shared with Apple or any third parties. This ensures that all personal media remains secure, providing users with peace of mind as they explore and utilize these advanced features.

A New Era of Media Management

Apple Intelligence's enhancements to photo and video search, combined with tools like Clean Up and Memories, set a new standard for media management and creativity. By leveraging natural language processing and advanced image recognition, Apple makes it easier than ever for users to find, perfect, and share their visual stories. This comprehensive approach ensures that users can enjoy a more intuitive, powerful, and private way to interact with their media, unlocking new possibilities for creativity and expression.

Part IV

A New Age For Siri

With the formidable capabilities of Apple Intelligence, Siri undergoes a transformative evolution, becoming more deeply integrated into the system experience than ever before. Armed with enhanced language-understanding capabilities, Siri now delivers interactions that are not only more natural but also more contextually relevant and deeply personalized.

Siri's newfound abilities simplify and expedite everyday tasks, ensuring a seamless user experience.

Seamless Interaction and Enhanced Understanding

Siri is now equipped to follow along if users stumble over words, maintaining context from one request to the next. This ensures smoother interactions and reduces the need for repeated commands. Moreover, users now have the option to type to Siri, seamlessly switching between text and voice communication based on their preference and the context of the moment.

Siri's redesigned interface features an elegant glowing light that wraps around the edge of the screen when active, providing visual feedback and enhancing the overall user experience.

Comprehensive Device Support and Expanded Knowledge Base

With Apple Intelligence, Siri offers comprehensive device support wherever users go, providing answers to thousands of questions about how to perform various tasks on iPhone, iPad, and Mac. From scheduling emails in the Mail app to toggling between Light and Dark Mode, Siri empowers users with invaluable guidance and assistance.

Enhanced Onscreen Awareness and Action Integration

Siri's onscreen awareness enables it to understand and take action with users' content in more apps over time. For instance, if a friend shares their new address in Messages, recipients can instruct Siri to automatically update the contact card with this information, streamlining the organization of personal data.

Expanded Actions Across Apple and Third-Party Apps

With Apple Intelligence, Siri gains the ability to execute hundreds of new actions across both Apple and third-party apps. Users can effortlessly issue commands such as "Retrieve the article about cicadas from my Reading List" or "Send the photos from Saturday's barbecue to Malia," and Siri will promptly execute the requested tasks, enhancing productivity and efficiency.

Tailored Intelligence and Seamless Access to Information

Siri delivers intelligence tailored to the user's preferences and on-device information. For instance, users can simply request Siri to "Play the podcast Jamie recommended," and Siri will locate and play the episode, eliminating the need for users to remember where the recommendation originated. Similarly, asking "When is Mom's flight landing?" prompts Siri to retrieve flight details and provide real-time tracking information for an estimated arrival time, ensuring users stay informed and organized effortlessly.

With Apple Intelligence powering Siri, users can expect a more intuitive, personalized, and seamless digital assistant experience, empowering them to accomplish tasks with unprecedented ease and efficiency

To ensure that Apple Intelligence truly delivers helpful insights while safeguarding user privacy, it relies on a deep understanding of personal context coupled with robust privacy measures. Central to this ethos is the concept of on-device processing, wherein many of the models powering Apple Intelligence operate entirely on the user's device. This approach not only ensures swift responsiveness but also minimizes the need for data to leave the device, thus enhancing privacy protection.

For more complex tasks requiring additional computational power, Apple introduces

Private Cloud Compute—an innovative solution that extends the privacy and security principles of Apple devices into the cloud, thereby unlocking even greater intelligence while preserving user privacy. With Private Cloud Compute, Apple Intelligence gains the flexibility to scale its computational capacity and leverage larger, server-based models for advanced requests.

These server-based models, powered by dedicated Apple silicon servers, form the backbone of Private Cloud Compute. Importantly, Apple ensures that data privacy remains paramount by never retaining or exposing user data. Independent experts have the opportunity to inspect the code running on Apple silicon servers, providing an additional layer of transparency and reassurance regarding privacy safeguards.

Moreover, Private Cloud Compute employs cryptographic measures to ensure that user devices—be it iPhone, iPad, or Mac—only communicate with servers whose software has been publicly logged for inspection. This rigorous verification process underscores Apple's commitment to transparency and privacy protection, setting a new industry standard for privacy in AI.

In essence, Apple Intelligence with Private Cloud Compute not only unlocks unprecedented levels of intelligence but also instills confidence in users by prioritizing their privacy and security. With this groundbreaking approach, Apple continues to lead the way in delivering trustworthy and privacy-centric AI solutions.

Part V

Apple & ChatGPT

Apple is integrating ChatGPT access directly into the core experiences of iOS 18, iPadOS 18, and macOS Sequoia, enabling users to leverage its expertise, image understanding, and document analysis capabilities seamlessly within their devices.

Siri, Apple's intelligent assistant, can now tap into ChatGPT's vast knowledge base to provide users with accurate and insightful responses to their queries. Before any questions are sent to ChatGPT, users are prompted for consent, ensuring transparency and control over their data. Siri then delivers the answer directly, streamlining the information retrieval process.

Moreover, ChatGPT will be integrated into Apple's systemwide Writing Tools, empowering users to generate content effortlessly across various contexts. With the Compose feature, users can access ChatGPT's image tools to create visuals in diverse styles, complementing their written content seamlessly.

Privacy is a top priority for Apple, and robust protections are built into the ChatGPT integration. Users' IP addresses are obscured, and OpenAI does not store requests. Furthermore, ChatGPT's stringent data-use policies apply, offering users peace of mind when accessing its capabilities.

ChatGPT will be rolled out to iOS 18, iPadOS 18, and macOS Sequoia later this year, powered by GPT-4o. Users can access ChatGPT for free without the need to create an account, while subscribers can connect their accounts to unlock additional paid features directly within these experiences. This integration marks a significant advancement in user accessibility to advanced AI capabilities, further enhancing the utility and versatility of Apple's ecosystem.

Availability

Apple Intelligence will be offered to users free of charge and will be available in beta as part of iOS 18, iPadOS 18, and macOS Sequoia starting this fall, initially in U.S. English. Over the course of the next year, additional features, software platforms, and languages will be introduced to enhance the user experience further.

Apple Intelligence will be compatible with iPhone 15 Pro, iPhone 15 Pro Max, iPad, and Mac devices equipped with M1 chipsets or later. Siri and device language settings must be set to U.S. English to access Apple Intelligence functionalities.

For more information and updates, users can visit apple.com/apple-intelligence.

About Apple:

Apple has been at the forefront of personal technology innovation since the introduction of the Macintosh in 1984. Today, Apple continues to lead the industry with groundbreaking products such as iPhone, iPad, Mac, AirPods, Apple Watch, and Apple Vision Pro. With six software platforms—iOS, iPadOS, macOS, watchOS, visionOS, and tvOS—Apple delivers seamless experiences across all its devices, providing users with access to breakthrough services including the App Store, Apple Music, Apple Pay, iCloud, and Apple TV+.

With a global team of over 150,000 employees, Apple remains committed to creating the best products on earth while also striving to leave the world a better place than they found it.

CONCLUSION

As we bring this exploration of Apple Intelligence to a close, we find ourselves standing at the precipice of a new era. This journey has taken us through the meticulous development and innovative integration of a platform that promises to reshape the way we interact with technology. Apple Intelligence is not just a technological marvel; it is a testament to human ingenuity and the relentless pursuit of progress.

Reflecting on the humble beginnings of artificial intelligence, it's remarkable to witness how far we've come. From the early days of simplistic, rule-based systems to the sophisticated, on-device AI modeling that powers Apple Intelligence, the evolution has been nothing short of extraordinary. This journey, punctuated by Apple's acquisition of Perceptio and their collaboration with OpenAI, showcases a commitment to pushing boundaries while preserving the core values of privacy and security.

Apple Intelligence stands as a beacon of what's possible when visionary thinking meets cutting-edge technology. The seamless integration across iOS 18, iPadOS 18, and macOS Sequoia, coupled with the empowering capabilities of ChatGPT, brings forth an era where our devices not only respond to our needs but anticipate them with a level of understanding previously thought unattainable.

As we look ahead, the promise of Apple Intelligence is more than just enhanced functionality; it is about transforming our relationship with technology into something more intuitive, personal, and profoundly human. Imagine a world where our devices become true companions, understanding our intentions, assisting us in ways that are deeply meaningful, and freeing us to focus on what truly matters.

In the grand tapestry of technological advancement, Apple Intelligence is a vibrant thread, weaving together innovation, empathy, and the human spirit. It reminds us that the ultimate goal of technology is to elevate our lives, making them richer, more connected, and more fulfilling. As we embrace this future, let us do so with the knowledge that we are not just adopting new tools, but embarking on a journey towards a more intelligent and compassionate world.

Thank you for joining us on this journey. May Apple Intelligence inspire you to dream bigger, reach higher, and embrace the future with open arms and an open heart.

www.ingramcontent.com/pod-product-compliance
Lightning Source LLC
Chambersburg PA
CBHW061053050326
40690CB00012B/2600